Violin part

the best of grade

Violin

A compilation of the best Grade 1 violin pieces ever selected by the major examination boards

Selected and edited by Jessica O'Leary

© 2012 by Faber Music Ltd
This edition first published in 2012
Bloomsbury House
74–77 Great Russell Street
London WC1B 3DA
Music processed by Jackie Leigh
Design by Økvik Design
Cover image: Stockbyte (skd282880sdc)
Printed in England by Caligraving Ltd

ISBN10: 0-571-53691-3
EAN13: 978-0-571-53691-7

To buy Faber Music publications or to find out about the full range of titles available
please contact your local music retailer or Faber Music sales enquiries:

Faber Music Limited, Burnt Mill, Elizabeth Way, Harlow CM20 2HX
Tel: +44 (0)1279 82 89 82   Fax: +44 (0)1279 82 89 83
sales@fabermusic.com   fabermusicstore.com

Audio tracks recorded at Barn Cottage Studio, July 2012
Performed by Jessica O'Leary (violin) and Robin Bigwood (piano)

Engineered by Robin Bigwood
℗ 2012 Faber Music Ltd © 2012 Faber Music Ltd

Contents

The following pieces are included in current Grade 1 examination syllabuses:
Rondeau (Purcell): LIST A, ABRSM 2012–15
Fly High, Pterodactyl (Lumsden/Wedgwood): LIST A, TRINITY 2010–15

The performers

Jessica O'Leary is a professional violinist, teacher, ABRSM examiner and seminar presenter. She has toured and recorded extensively as a member of the Academy of St Martin in the Fields, and has performed with Madonna, Led Zeppelin, the London Symphony Orchestra and the Royal Opera House.

Robin Bigwood is a freelance pianist and harpsichordist, performing with Passacaglia, Feinstein Ensemble, Britten Sinfonia and as a soloist. He also works as a sound engineer and producer.

Track 1: Tuning note A

Fanfare

from 'The Young Violinist's Repertoire Book 1'

PERFORMANCE 2
ACCOMPANIMENT 3

Create an exciting military feel by keeping strict time and using stark dynamic contrasts.
In the loud sections use full bows for the crotchets and quarter-bows for the quavers.

Michel Corrette (1709–1795)
arr. de Keyser and Waterman

Allegro [♩ = 120]

f

FINE

p

mf

D.C. al Fine

Rondeau

from 'Superstart Violin'

PERFORMANCE 4
ACCOMPANIMENT 5

This is an elegant piece that uses lots of different bow lengths. Try lifting your bow at the end of phrases to give a dance-like character.

Henry Purcell (1659–1695)
arr. Cohen and Spearing

The Grey Dove

from 'The Young Violinist's Repertoire Book 1'

The slurs and 4th fingers help make this a spirited piece. Lift your bow in the air just before the last note to lead in your accompanist for an exciting finish!

PERFORMANCE 6
ACCOMPANIMENT 7

Ignacy Komarovsky (1824–1857)
arr. de Keyser and Waterman

Noel Nouvelet

from 'The Young Violinist's Early Music Collection'

PERFORMANCE 8
ACCOMPANIMENT 9

This is a great performance piece with a strong rhythm and sense of purpose. Use tiny bows for the semiquavers so they don't stick out.

anon. 15th-century French
arr. Edward Huws Jones

Rhythmic, but not fast ♩ = 72

March from 'Scipio'

This is the regimental march of the Grenadier Guards. For fun, see if you can memorise it and play while walking!

George Frideric Handel (1685–1759)

arr. Jessica O'Leary

Slovak Song

from 'Violin Playtime Book 2'

This is a bubbly piece with exciting piano parts, so smile at your pianist when you are ready to start. At the end, stand tall until the whole piece is over and then take a big bow!

trad.
arr. Paul de Keyser

From Old Vienna

from 'Violin Playtime Book 3'

This piece changes speed, so watch out for the Italian words that signal tempo changes.
A good left-hand position will help the 2nd finger move higher and then lower more easily.

anon.
arr. Paul de Keyser

Waltz from 'The Merry Widow'

from 'Going Solo'

PERFORMANCE 16
ACCOMPANIMENT 17

Play this famous waltz with full bows to help the melody sing out. Sneak in the separate
crotchets in bars 17, 21, 25 and 27 with tiny bows to keep the music flowing.

Franz Lehár (1870–1948)
arr. Edward Huws Jones

Waltz moderato ♩ = 112

Land of the Silver Birch

from 'O Shenandoah!'

The open strings get the music off to a strong start. Use lots of bow in the loud sections and exaggerate the dynamic contrasts for dramatic effect.

trad.
arr. Waterfield and Beach

Largo from the New World Symphony

from 'Superstart Violin'

The bow should be tilted throughout to make a glossy sound. Place your bow over the fingerboard for the very quiet phrases; use plenty of bow here, but play lightly, as though you have a helium balloon under your right arm!

Antonin Dvořák (1841–1904)
arr. Cohen and Spearing

What shall we do with the Drunken Sailor?

from 'Up-Grade! 1–2'

PERFORMANCE 22
ACCOMPANIMENT 23

The bowing needs to flow along quickly and smoothly, so only use the middle part. Start by playing the rhythm of the first bar on a G major scale to see how little bow you need.

trad.
arr. Pam Wedgwood

As fast as possible [♩ = 88]

Fly High, Pterodactyl

from 'Jurassic Blue'

This tune has great words that reflect the character and rhythm of the music. Aim to use small bows for the quavers to keep the music flowing along and be bold with the dynamics for drama!

Caroline Lumsden
and Pam Wedgwood

At a steady speed ♩ = 108

f Fly high, Pte - ro - dac - tyl, fly high with

me, fly high o - ver cliff tops, we'll reach the

sea. *mp* Fly high, Pte - ro - dac - tyl, with ti - ny

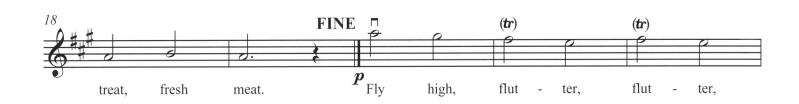

feet, *f* let's search for some din - ner, I'd like a

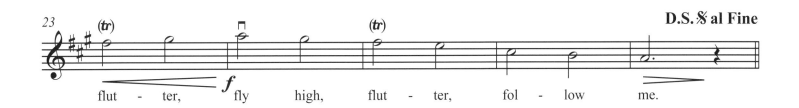

treat, fresh meat. *p* Fly high, flut - ter, flut - ter,

flut - ter, *f* fly high, flut - ter, fol - low me.

Elenke

from 'Gypsy Jazz (Easy Level)'

PERFORMANCE 26
ACCOMPANIMENT 27

This lively piece has lots of open strings and strong separate bowing in the loud passages.
Use small bows for the slurs in the quiet phrases to create a sense of contrast.

trad. Bulgarian
arr. Polly Waterfield

Oh, Lady, Be Good

This is great jazz piece and the rhythms will seem easy if you feel the music in two big beats per bar. For fun, try clapping the tune while you tap the beats with your foot!

Music and Lyrics by
George Gershwin and Ira Gershwin

Sharks

from 'Going Solo'

This is a dramatic piece that needs full and strong tone. Make sure your bow is parallel to the bridge throughout, then whisk it into the air at the very end to finish in style!

Edward Huws Jones

PERFORMANCE 30
ACCOMPANIMENT 31